Expressive Interiors

Expressive Interiors

DESIGNING AN INVITING HOME

Sandra Lucas and Sarah Eilers

LUCAS/EILERS DESIGN ASSOCIATES

with Judith Nasatir
Principal photography by Stephen Karlisch

RIZZOLI
NEW YORK

New York · Paris · London · Milan

To:

Our mothers, who have always inspired us,
Our husbands, who encourage us,
Our children, who amaze us,

And our clients, friends, and colleagues,
who challenge and support us.

We are grateful for you all.

TABLE OF CONTENTS

INTRODUCTION

Every waking hour, and often in our dreams, Sandy and I live and breathe design. We are passionate about creating memorable, unique, welcoming residences that express their owners' personalities and suit their individual lifestyles. As classically trained designers, we have spent the past forty years putting the basic principles and elements of design to work every day to create beautifully balanced, wonderfully comfortable rooms that function with ease and elegance. We know the rules. We love the rules. And we love to break the rules. Interior design guides our lives. This spirit animates the following pages.

Sarah and I founded our Houston, Texas–based firm in 1995. Since then, we believe we have developed a distinctive philosophy and aesthetic—a friendly, compelling, persuasive "third coast" approach—that combines the entrepreneurial grit of the West, the charm and traditions of the South, and the diversity of a large metropolitan city. As native Houstonians, we have spent our lives absorbing the distinctive influences of our hometown and incorporating them with inspiration from our travels around the country and the world. The contemporary art collections of the de Menils, the traditional architecture of John F. Staub, and the textures of the surrounding ranches and landscapes along with the postmodern impact of NASA are just a few aspects of Houston's design world and culture that have guided our decision-making in the homes we have designed from coast to coast.

What binds us together is a respect for design, for each other's distinctive aesthetic, and for our clients, both young and older. We share the idea that good design is . . . good design. We like to think that everything we do is timeless. We also like to make things fun and relevant. But above all, we love balance, both asymmetrical and symmetrical. We take a pragmatic, practical, and, we hope,

PAGE 2: Rustic meets refined in this cozy inglenook with a landscape painting by Stephen Hannock. PAGE 5: A juxtaposition of textures and ample light create a wonderful spot for reading. PAGE 6: This color palette brings the outdoors inside and gives the blue-and-white porcelain a fresh feel. OPPOSITE: With a mix of old and new, this entry introduces the aesthetic that follows.

poetic approach to space planning and interiors. We are guided by the importance of context and suitability. We know the power of scale and proportion. We understand the science and emotion of color and light. We delight in playing with the effects of patterns and textures. We believe that art and accessories are what make each room complete. In our view, these classical design principles and elements are the profession's sine qua non.

We met as sorority sisters at the University of Texas at Austin. Sandy was already a design major. I was planning to be. From the beginning, we knew we had a lot in common. This was even before we shared the experiences of staying up all night drafting projects by hand, interning for architectural firms, and seeking out and learning from wonderful mentors in design.

By nature, we are both rule followers. We find it hard to look at an Empire chair and not envision it upholstered in a Napoleonic Bee fabric, at least initially. But what fun it is to do the unexpected: to use oversized patterns and other-than-predictable colors on antique chairs, to arrange a mixed rather than matching set of dining chairs around a table, to place a bed or a sofa against a window instead of a solid wall.

We live by the motto: "There are no problems . . . only design opportunities." Experience has taught us that our profession is filled with Murphy's Law situations. Even with the best-laid plans, we know we will need to make decisions and alterations in the field. And so we embrace the challenges. For all the years we have spent honing our individual skills and seizing opportunities that have come our way, we still believe that two heads are better than one. Sarah and I regularly consult with each other when we are stumped on a project. We have always helped one another with our own homes. We know we each benefit not only from the other's fresh set of eyes, but also from our different points of view, that individual cast of mind that perceives what we see in another light.

Sarah and I grew up in the same neighborhood and with the same circle of friends, but our families were very different. Sarah's were collectors, so from

OPPOSITE: Various textures combine with smooth plaster walls and wood plank floors and ceiling to create a warm, inviting breakfast room. Grass shades soften the light and add privacy without completely obscuring the views. An antique chandelier hovers over the center table; the form of its iron base echoes the distinctive carved frames of the antique French mutton-bone chairs.

childhood she has appreciated and lived with beautiful antiques. My family was much more modest in design, but my mother loved the latest trends and changed the rooms of our home constantly. She would make the absolute most of her design budget, and she did work regularly with a designer. I still remember coming home from school one day to find the shock of the new: our family room redone in the bright orange and turquoise that I imagined to be the Rob and Laura Petrie look—mid-century modern, in the mid-century.

Unlike Sandy's more contemporary interiors, the aesthetic in my home was very traditional. Both sets of my grandparents had worked with Doris Duckworth, Houston's leading decorator in those days. Even before my father met my mother, he focused on design. I still have a newspaper article that named him one of Houston's most eligible young bachelors; the accompanying photograph shows him with his collections of pine antiques and china. After they married, my parents collected American and English antiques. When they built the house I grew up in, they worked with a designer and purchased some fantastic pieces. They also had a farm filled with wonderful antiques.

The nature and culture of our design backgrounds are evident in everything we do, from what we collect to the way we have designed our own homes to the way we approach our projects—I tend to start by selecting the rugs, while Sandy always considers the art first—to the interiors of our offices at the firm. Mine has an old-world partners desk and a pair of Queen Anne chairs that were in my father's office. Sandy's space is sleeker and more contemporary, with a clean-lined laminate worktable/desk that she designed for function first. We both have Aeron chairs, and the same bulletin boards. But my bulletin board, which hangs horizontally, is neat, with things pinned in regimental order. Sandy's is vertical, with things placed very haphazardly. Creativity and good design have many faces.

OPPOSITE: In the Lucas home, a beech wood goat found in Paris moves from room to room as a conversation point. A seventeenth-century English sideboard with linen-fold panels and a converted antique candle-stand lamp with a linen shade offer interesting textural contrasts to the brick floor. Hand-hewn floating shelves provide storage and display space.

When we studied the principles and elements of design, and the theory and history of design, they were at first academic ideas we needed to learn and absorb. Now, after years of experience, they are the practical knowledge behind the design—and our approach to creating rooms that work—and the reason for structuring this book as we have. In the first half, we explain our fresh take on the rules with chapters on planning, context and suitability, scale and proportion, color and light, pattern and texture, and art and collections. In the second half, we tour you through homes we have designed from coast to coast, through rooms where we have followed the rules, and through rooms where we have rewritten them. Because we both believe that mistakes are great teachers, we often test and refine new ideas on ourselves before we explore them with clients. The final section, Design Laboratory, gives you a glimpse into what that means in our homes.

To celebrate the twentieth anniversary of our firm, we designed a house for Habitat for Humanity. Clearly, the parameters were different than those of our usual clients. Yet the challenge and the approach we took to it were the same: to make each space the absolute best it could be. In other words, we boiled the interiors down to our essential belief in design's power to change people's lives house by house, room by room, space by space.

It is still so common to think of interior design as a matter of style. And it is. But it is also so much more. Making rooms function well is usually our primary goal. Everything else is gravy. This is why we emphasize the importance of classical design training, tempered and fine-tuned by years of experience. Does the room's traffic pattern create an easy flow? Is the lighting pleasing, warm, inviting, and flexible enough to change the mood? Do the furniture arrangements promote conversation and comfort? How does the house make you feel? And how do you want it to make others feel? In terms of the principles and elements of design, and the theory and history of design, these questions are basic and academic. In creating a home, and in rooms that work, they are anything but.

OPPOSITE: As longtime garden club members, fresh flowers, greenery, and plants are integral to our design approach. We always use native species along with cuttings from our clients' gardens to enhance their different rooms. A favorite antique porcelain bowl filled with airy blooms could not be more fitting for a table set with antique silver and crystal.

PART I
BEHIND THE DESIGN

esign has many right answers. "Because I said so" is never one of them. Creating a room that works—that is comfortable, beautiful, and personal—is all about organization and order. The process involves countless choices. The elements and principles of interior design give us the framework to sort through the possibilities, select what is best for the purpose, and explain the choices to others.

Definitions matter. The elements of design—space, line, shape, form, color, value, and texture—are the basics, the essence of everything we look at and touch in an interior. The principles—balance, unity, contrast, emphasis, pattern, scale, proportion, and rhythm—are the way we employ and combine the elements to achieve a desired design effect. Selecting a favorite element or principle is like being asked to pick a favorite child. Each is wonderful in its own way. Good design arranges the elements into a unifying, visual order. It is the logic behind the relationships that ensures the interior landscape becomes not a battle of wills as such, but more like a symphony of the elements. After years in practice, we do this instinctively.

Each room, and every home, is by definition its own unique puzzle. Before we start, we try to determine what will be the most important element, or the detail that will make the greatest impact. Every step of the way, we continue to think through them. The process is a little like doing a sudoku. Every choice informs the next. And ultimately the pieces fall into place like building blocks.

This book explores the design elements we use most, as well as the critical details that are important to each project. The order of the chapters provides a guideline of how we organize the design process. Planning comes first. Then we address matters of context and suitability, scale and proportion, and color and light. The issues of pattern and texture follow next. We finish up with the details of art and collections, though we like to think about these final components from the very beginning. Our goal is always to find the most practical, artistic, personal combination of all the elements and details—because that is what makes a room work.

PLANNING

Unrolling a new set of plans is like Christmas morning. There is nothing more fun or exciting than those first hours of sitting and studying the different rooms, mentally walking through the entire home, imagining the possibilities, sketching furniture arrangements, and then adding ideas for art and details to the elevations. We initially focus on the interior's fixed architectural elements, "the bones." These include not only the ceiling height, windows, doors, fireplace, walls, and stairways, but also the way the spaces flow into one another. Ample natural light, good circulation, and thoughtful positioning factor significantly into every design equation, whether of a good room or a great home. These are the essential components, the aspects of architecture that make up the intrinsic character of the space. Sometimes, adjustments are necessary. Sometimes, not. We love good bones. We are grateful for good architecture.

The advantage of building a house from the ground up is that the design begins with fewer limitations so the chance of realizing the dream seems that much greater. But parameters always exist. Bigger is not always better. Common sense is still involved. We also love historic preservation. If there are reasons to save a project, that is always our first choice. We weigh the pros and the cons. Typically, we insist that the homeowner bring in an architect to help make a thoroughly informed decision as to whether or not it is better to renovate or start from scratch.

To make the absolute most of a given space and a particular design, it is critical for us to think through every aspect and detail in the planning stages, while everything is still on paper or the computer screen. This is the time when it is still possible and comparatively easy to change, reset, and improve the bones, if necessary. We work to refine the dimensions of each room to the inch: to consider window and door sizes and locations for the best possible views, light, and flow; to make sure

OPPOSITE: In this renovated foyer, ashlar-patterned bluestone pavers, like those on the exterior patios, and a fiddle-leaf fig tree in an olive jar reinforce the indoor/outdoor connection. An early nineteenth-century mirror over the antique Italian console brings the interior and exterior together through its reflection of the entry terrace plantings and fountain.

Some couples have very different ideas about what a particular space should look like. The designer's challenge is to think differently because there is always another option: a design with elements that please both.

RIGHT: Both members of this couple love this library, which seems to marry the differences between masculine and feminine aesthetics. Millwork painted a soft taupe keeps the space fresh, light, and airy, as the wife wished. Dark-stained, V-groove paneling in the back of the bookcases gives it the depth that the husband desired. Plaster walls and a strong stone fireplace mantel enhance the effect. The rug, a monochromatic Oushak designed to look old, inspired the soft color palette.

RIGHT: Donald Sultan's *Smoke Rings* creates the focal point for this living room in Virginia. Flanking it, antique fragments turned into sconces comment on the painting's complex curves with a flourish, as does the hand-carved stone mantel found on a buying trip to France. Antique French walnut doors introduce the warmth of wood. The mango tones of the niche and ceiling sunnily complement the room's dark woods and metals.

RIGHT: This Texas-sized living room is an addition, part of the remodel of a 1970s ranch house inherited and shared by two brothers. The planked, beamed ceiling refers directly to the house's history. The custom, mohair-covered sofas—each more than one hundred inches long to fit the room's scale—accommodate all the family members who gather here. The custom cabinet meets the sofa's dimensions with spirit. A large-screen television lifts out of the console, which also serves as a transition to the kitchen.

the art walls are sufficient; to factor in allowances for incorporating architectural antiques, such as mantels, if that is the homeowner's desire.

Knowing where to look and how to move into and through each room is an essential part of creating comfort. The best rooms have clear primary and secondary focal points—views, a fireplace, a doorway—that orient the person within them. When a room lacks these visual cues, it falls to us to create them and establish a clear hierarchy of importance.

Occasionally, when we look at the plans, our first instinct is to arrange the furnishings in a specific room in a certain way. It seems clear, even obvious, where the focal point should be, and all the other elements and groupings that should follow from it. It sometimes happens, though, that in doing this, we may miss an even better solution. The more opportunity and time we have to study and work on a plan, the better it is for everyone. When we start our collaboration, the clients might have their minds set on how they expect to use the particular space. As we begin to talk through and analyze the various options, unexpected solutions can come to mind that may provide something special that all of us will have overlooked at the first glance.

Everyone today asks for rooms that are multifunctional and as open as possible. Everyone today wants every inch of their interiors to be useful, comfortable, and accessible to the entire family: to children, grandchildren, and pets. From our perspective, that means the rooms we design need to serve their purpose elegantly. We want each to be distinctive, yet contribute to a unifying aesthetic so the many spaces flow seamlessly together. We love thinking outside of the box. We cherish creativity. The more challenging the puzzle, the better. But what drives us most of all is creativity in the service of function, comfort, and beauty. Rooms need to work.

OPPOSITE: All the elements of this dining room play off its groin-vaulted ceiling. The room comes together around the rug, with a pattern that subtly echoes the architecture overhead. An antique gilded mirror above a Directoire chest balances the opening to the kitchen. The table is a handcrafted piece by Keith Fritz. A gilded wood, crystal, and iron chandelier adds sparkle without being too fussy. Along the wall, an antique bench grounds a large, dramatic canvas by Joseph Adolphe.

RIGHT: This symmetrical, modern kitchen, part of an addition by architect Dillon Kyle for a Houston home built in 1939, is firmly grounded in tradition but designed for today's way of living. The wood floor is in the style of the original house for continuity. The panel details of the cabinetry also echo the existing interiors. Painted white for brightness, the V-groove ceiling infuses the space with more woody warmth. The finishes and palette may be simple and understated, but the materials, including the Carrara marble counters, are elegant, fresh, and timeless. Pendant lights with custom-colored shades help to define the island's workspace.

ABOVE: A utility room off the kitchen's back hallway continues the color palette but incorporates a bluestone floor for more durability. OPPOSITE: The view from the kitchen's farmhouse sink overlooks the pool. The Roman shade's patterned fabric from F. Schumacher brings in references from the garden. Upholstered counter stools with arms are especially comfortable for casual gatherings around the island while meal preparation is underway.

There are countless creative ways to conceal a TV so that it does not distract from the beauty of the room when not in use. Out of sight is out of mind.

RIGHT: When the owners of this house were transforming an adjacent guest bedroom into this new master sitting room, they had already decided they wanted it to include a large-screen TV. That said, the space originally lacked a focal point. The mural wallpaper by Barry Dixon for Vervain, which makes art of the TV cabinet doors, addressed both needs beautifully. Cladding the vaulted ceiling in natural wood with complementary pale tones brought in a soft organic texture that enhanced the room's calmness.

RIGHT: We were brought on board midway through construction, so it made perfect sense to use an open plan for this kitchen because the workspace unfolded on the left into the breakfast room. The homeowners requested this shade of blue, and Segreto Finishes of Houston developed a glaze that softened and enriched the color's effect. Quartzite counters and light-colored stools add contrast, as does the patterned tile behind the cook top.

CONTEXT
AND SUITABILITY

At the outset of many projects, people ask us: "What's popular today?" We can show them the look of the moment. We can analyze and explain all of its components. But our goal is different. We aspire to create interiors that our clients will love today and that will still be timely and right for them years from now. This is why the classical rules of context and suitability—the common-sense aspects of design—matter so much. Both are key to determining comfort and style because they connect the dots of all the choices to function, geographic location, and the homeowner's dreams and ideas. Keeping them front of mind throughout the decision-making process helps us create rooms and homes that are not only personal and unique but also timeless—and that fit like the proverbial glove.

We all know immediately when we walk into rooms that really work. We can see and feel the appropriateness of the choices: every selection is what it should be, where it should be, and why it should be. This is not to say that such rooms can't include some "wow" factors. They can. And they often do. These design decisions that surprise and delight us may involve color, pattern, texture, individual furnishings, artwork, or creative architectural elements. What matters is that even as they capture our attention, they still relate clearly to the room's function and surroundings—and to the exterior landscape as well as the interior landscape of adjacent spaces.

Mixing styles and periods is a favorite way to make a home unique and elegant. Yes, a red-brick Georgian can have a contemporary interior. A modern structure can certainly welcome antiques. The implementation of context and suitability is what makes a mix successful and a home interesting yet balanced and well-organized.

OPPOSITE: As part of the remodel of this family ranch outside Houston, architect Natalye Appel added a long porch of wood and stone that opens off the living room. Fitting comfortably under the lean-to-style roof, a custom lantern features an open framework that prevents the native birds from using it to nest.

Although we do not like to do the obvious, we do like to thoughtfully keep in mind the location, climate, and atmosphere of each project. Whether it is a local/ native natural stone used in a ranch house in Texas or tabby used for a second home in South Carolina, we strive to take advantage of the local color and flavor of the surroundings. Using regional craftsmen and artists allows us to not only support the neighboring community but also create a home that fits naturally into the environment. As members of the design team for a home on a ten-acre property in the mountains, we walked the property to determine the best placement and orientation. We spotted owl feathers and arrowheads, along with trees and plants that inspired the design for our interiors.

Rules are made to be broken, of course. We feel that it is our job to explain the "rules" and then explain how to successfully break them. Many interiors shown in today's shelter magazines seem to have decisions made simply for shock value. Like chocolate and vanilla, there are designs that appeal to everyone. We love clients with opinions; the collaboration is what leads to great designs that work.

The challenge is to find a comfort level with rule bending, and decide which boundaries to push. Some homeowners want to stretch them more than others, and in different areas. Maybe they want the art to be a little more dramatic. Or they could prefer to make more of a statement with the architecture, the color, or the scale. Most of our designs tend to the more conservative side, and are quite edited to our clients' wishes. Most of the people we design for want to invest in good art and in high-quality furnishings and finishes. For that reason, they do not want to take a chance that they will tire of those decisions quickly. Making a home livable is very important. This is why we advise people to think about what they love and what will be comfortable and classic for them long-term, regardless of what that is. Interiors that work are interiors that endure.

OPPOSITE: Part of the original architecture, the ranch's dining room is awash in natural light during the day. For night, cable lights supplement the hanging fixture, an antique scale transformed with LED candles in different heights, which balances the room's vast proportions. The fabric on the chair backs pulls colors from the living room rug.

ABOVE: Made from a downed tree found on the property, a live-edge shelf spanning the length of the kitchen provides storage without obscuring the views. Wall-mounted fixtures on every column make sure that the room is well lit when the sun sets.
OPPOSITE: The vaulted ceiling, part of the renovation, now matches that of the dining area. Two granite sinks center workspaces that easily accommodate more than one cook. A pot rack inspired the cooktop's custom hood, which also incorporates lighting.

RIGHT: The screened porch of this vacation house on Kiawah Island looks out to palm trees and a lagoon. For alfresco dining, lightweight galvanized metal chairs are easy to move when the number of diners increases. A gray stained teak trestle table adds to the overall feeling of lightness, but offers ultimate durability for the salt air and humidity of the island's climate.

42

ABOVE: In this historic home renovated for avid collectors of American antiques, a bronze death mask of Abraham Lincoln hangs above a period burl-wood chest; another, of George Washington, commands the flanking wall. OPPOSITE: A round table worked perfectly in this essentially square dining room. Because the walls left no space for storage or serving, corner niches designed with the architect now display the clients' extensive collection of white ironstone china. A custom, hand-painted scenic wallpaper depicts Houston's Hermann Park, where the homeowners walk their dog daily.

Adding multiple structures rather
than building the necessary
space under one roof can create
a challenge to visual consistency.
Pulling design elements from
the surroundings ensures
that all the spaces relate, even
when their functions differ.

RIGHT: This large party room, one of multiple additions to a renovated Texas farmhouse,
incorporates colors and materials from other structures on the property. The specific
shade of red on the ceiling and the barn door (as well as the door itself) pick up on aspects
of the property's reconstructed Amish barn and the hue that this family farm has used for
decades. The stone and reclaimed timbers establish a consistent framework throughout.

ABOVE: On the Lucas patio, hand-forged wing chairs from Formations provide a place for cozy conversation. Created around an iron serpent spout found on the property at the time of purchase, the fountain works well with the reclaimed brick and other materials. OPPOSITE: Designed for relaxation and closeness to the outdoors, the family room of this vacation house on Kiawah Island incorporates a mix of contemporary pieces and antiques found in nearby Charleston.

ABOVE: Raffia placemats with a shell fringe, sage-colored napkins, and the owner's saltware give this table setting a sense of place. OPPOSITE: The long dining table creates a functional transition area between the living room and kitchen. With a bench on one side and occasional chairs on the other, it accommodates small and large groups. FOLLOWING SPREAD: This outdoor Texas living room focuses on views of the pool and Brazos River Valley. Easy-to-rearrange teak furnishings hold up beautifully in the climate.

SCALE AND PROPORTION

In *Running with Scissors*, a very moving memoir by Augusten Burroughs, the author writes at one point, "I hate this kitchen. I need high ceilings." We empathize. Every human being reacts physically and emotionally to rooms the instant we walk into them. The source of that primal feeling of comfort or discomfort, though, can be difficult to define or analyze without understanding scale and proportion. These two fundamental elements of design are why good design is much more of a numbers game than most people realize. *Scale* refers to the size of an entire object in relationship to another entire object. *Proportion* refers to the relative size of parts of a whole. There is one other classical mathematical formula for beauty: the golden ratio or golden section, which is nature's ideal of relativity, the comparative relationships that delight the eye with their rightness. (Technically, you find the golden ratio by dividing a length into two so that the longer part divided by the smaller part is also equal to the entire length divided by the longer part.) In all the rooms that we design, and every custom piece as well, we work scale, proportion, and the golden ratio to the nth degree.

All humans comprehend the scale and proportion of the elements in and of our surroundings through the way they relate to our bodies—in other words, in terms of human scale. One house might have a nine-foot ceiling height. In another, the ceilings might be twelve feet. If we do not factor the body's proportions into the elevation as we begin to plan the room's layout and contents, the potential for mistakes is enormous. The furniture could feel like doll furniture. Or the room might seem like the Jolly Green Giant lives there. But if the scale and proportions are right from the start, the completed space will feel effortless and comfortable to the eye.

OPPOSITE: The owners of this Houston home wanted a large-scale scenic pattern in their twelve-foot-high dining room. We commissioned a local artist to create a design of dogwoods and native Texas birds that brought the walls to life; the pattern takes cues from the natural surroundings and the colors of the rug.

RIGHT: Designed to connect an existing house with the newly added spaces, this loggia is intended to look like an exterior porch that was enclosed at a later date. The combination of materials—painted brick, bluestone, wood beams, and a V-groove ceiling—helps break up the space to define its scale and proportion. Carefully sized custom lanterns fit the volume. The generously dimensioned antique vitrine feels right at home.

As we draw floor plans and furniture layouts, we use markers with a more or less generic scale—a seven-foot sofa, thirty-nine inches deep, for example—to stand in for the pieces that will come. Once we have made all the selections, we go back, measure the exact dimensions of the items, and put them into the plan to make sure they work. Design school does not prepare you for how much math and geometry there is in design. If you opt for a round dining table, dividing its circumference (found by multiplying pi by its diameter) by the dimensions/number of chairs is the only way to calculate accurately how many chairs will fit around the table without squishing. And you must be able to slide the chairs under the table. An inch can make an enormous difference in so many decisions. Just think of those living rooms where the coffee table is too large, making it almost impossible to slip past it to the sofa; or too far away to easily set your cocktail down. More math!

Sometimes we very purposefully make a choice that is unexpected in scale or proportion because it adds interest. Perhaps more importantly, playing with scale and proportion can resolve some otherwise difficult spatial challenges. Decisions about lighting illustrate what we mean. A very small light fixture in a large space—or conversely, a very large fixture in a small space—can add a happy element of surprise. But there is more to it than that. As a rule, we prefer to use recessed lights sparingly. (There are many instances, such as in some high rises with concrete ceilings, where we simply cannot.) Of course, it may be possible to lower the ceiling to add recessed lighting; even then, we prefer a decorative option. We might decide to span the room with a custom fixture so that its scale meets the room's scale. With a vaulted ceiling, we also might opt for a lighting element that is similarly surprising in scale so it becomes not just a pretty piece of the décor, but a functional focal point that humanizes the volume. As long as the fixture's form, line, materials, and color are appropriate to its surroundings, it will be, too, no matter its scale and proportions. When all the principles and elements of design start marrying together and aligning in purpose, the room will work.

OPPOSITE: For this small sitting area, custom seating features backs a bit higher than normal to complement the ceiling height. Artworks by Reuben Nakian stacked over the settee fit the room's scale and proportion. FOLLOWING SPREAD: Because the living room's angled ceiling and high dormer windows ruled out recessed lights, we designed an oversized custom chandelier in collaboration with the architect to light the expansive space beautifully and evenly.

ABOVE: Hunt Slonem's bunnies over the tree-branch console add a bit of bold whimsy to an intimate corner of this Virginia living room, contrasting nicely with the intricate Holland & Sherry embroidery on the draperies. Window seats add extra cozy spots for reading. OPPOSITE: In this renovation, the steel and glass panels that replaced smaller, double-hung windows changed the scale of the room enough to balance the large pieces and artwork the homeowners brought from their prior, more spacious residence.

OPPOSITE: In the master bedroom of a Texas ranch house, a reclaimed beam set at the spot where the ceiling height changes creates a very comfortable seating nook. Drapery panels that go all the way to the ceiling give this lower portion of the room a vertical lift. The chairs have a slightly higher back to suit the room's proportions.
ABOVE: The area over the eighteenth-century mantel called for artwork of a certain scale, proportion, and feeling. This painting of cottonwoods commissioned from Clay Wagstaff suited the purpose perfectly.

COLOR AND LIGHT

We love old movies for so many reasons. But as interior designers, we cannot help but watch them for the sets. Like the artists behind the camera, we use color and light to create mood and express personality. We love how these two most mysterious elements of design play off each other, their surroundings, and the people who live in the rooms.

Color is endlessly variable in terms of value, hue, and intensity. Light is the same, and even more difficult to pin down. Because all of us react to what we see both physically and emotionally—and because our descriptive language so often falls short—it is important to get very specific rather than taking people's favorites at face value. A warm dark gray feels different than a cool dark gray. Brick and carmine, though both red, are as distinctive as chalk and cheese.

Clients rarely come to us with a particular palette in mind. New or existing finishes, art, and rugs influence the choices, which is why we like to have a good handle on these items early in the project. But inspiration, so important and difficult to predict, can strike at any time, from anywhere. There is nothing quite like the thrill of the "Eureka!" moment—that instant when, after all the listening, searching, and imagining about what could be, a concrete idea suddenly appears. It talks to you. Everybody gets goose bumps. And the direction is clear.

We find that when the whole house is done in a similar hue, it becomes much easier to get a feeling for the entirety of the house, not just the individual rooms. It is also amazing how much larger spaces look with the thread of constant trim and paint colors. Even so, we always create some special rooms—libraries, dining rooms, entries, powder rooms—that stand out from the rest. The challenge in these spaces is to find that delicate balance, to walk that tightrope walk of interest, contrast, and balance.

OPPOSITE: In this Houston breakfast room, daylight is an energizing force. Wool challis sheers soften the sun's beams and also create privacy when needed. Pressed ferns on one wall bring in the garden beyond the French doors. Dark wood accents and the chair fabric's overscaled arabesque pattern balance the room's more ethereal elements.

In a very neutral shell, punches and blocks of color in the art, the rugs, the pillows, the chairs, or the accessories add flair and increase the emotional temperature. If a house lacks compelling architectural features, color can help correct this. A Fortuny-like pattern in a metallic bronze can endow a small entry with a regal quality when appropriate. A floral wallpaper in bold reds, greens, and yellows can fill a dining room with whimsy when that suits. Making a home, especially an older home, more livable for today's lifestyle often involves opening rooms up to one another. In the end, this tends to mean fewer walls. Adding color to the ceiling, which we often think of as the fifth wall, can be the perfect way to resolve this issue.

The world outside the windows affects our perceptions of what is inside. We like to test and balance this calculus in real-life conditions, so we always do the initial color palettes in the office but take the boards to the job site to see how they look in natural light at morning, noon, and dusk. If there is a lot of green outside, it reflects into the space. If there is snow, sunlight seems to pick up in intensity as it bounces off the whiteness. Mountain light is always much clearer than city light, and so on. Our first choice is to have as much natural light as possible. Of course, this only works in the daytime, so we have to supplement it. The eternal question is how. We like to use as many different types of illumination as possible, balancing all the different sources available: pendants, lamps, sconces, flush mounts, recessed, and track, then using dimmers to control the mood.

There have been so many studies on the art and science of color and light, dating to long before Isaac Newton developed the color wheel we still use today, but lighting technology continues to change almost daily. And today's latest developments—colored gels along with a range of Kelvin temperatures and a CRI (color rendering index) that can warm the light sources up or cool them down—bring us back full circle to the old movie sets.

OPPOSITE: This living room's palette of soft greens and corals, derived from the rug's color scheme, contrasts beautifully with the homeowner's collection of cream pottery. Simple iron curtain rods pick up on the base of the glass-topped coffee table, which appears to float weightlessly on sleek legs with delicately hooved feet.

RIGHT: Concealed, motorized shades control the power of the sun while draperies provide softness in the living room of this Austin high rise. Diego Giacometti-inspired custom light fixtures marry the living and dining areas of the open floor plan. Vintage Art Deco chairs, the nesting coffee table, and the dining table base introduce lean lines that contrast with more substantial upholstered pieces.

ABOVE: A wall-sized painting of lilies commissioned from Joseph Adolphe features a color palette selected to enhance the soft greens in this space. **OPPOSITE**: With the palest of pale blue plaster on the walls and ceiling, this sitting room feels like the sanctuary it is meant to be. The tape at the hem of the upholstery pieces inserts a more saturated blue tone into the neutrals. On the walls, a series of lithographs by Leslie Parke titled *Almond Tree Reflection* repeats the same image in different colorations.

RIGHT: In this kitchen renovation, white and subtle neutrals prevail, even on the floating shelves that replaced closed cabinets. Different shades of blues in the ceiling, a quartzite island countertop, and leather stools add depth and contrast. Perched on the ledge of the range hood, a pair of plaster sculptures from the Marché aux Puces, the celebrated Paris flea market, introduces a playful note.

ABOVE: Design is always about the details, like the contrasting cord and frog that give such personality to this ottoman. OPPOSITE: Framing the V-groove walls with contrasting trim makes this bright family room feel even more fresh and inviting. The custom-colored print on the lounge chairs brings in the outdoors with its plant and animal motifs.

ABOVE: In this bedroom, the vase atop an antique walnut chest picks up on the blue wash that gives the headboard its presence. Brass hardware and details add shine and contrast. OPPOSITE: Plaster walls, an elegant rug, Fortuny bedding, and Venetian glass lamps set the stage in this master bedroom. An antique, hand-gilded bed crown with drapes and a sunburst mirror add even more drama to the four-poster bed.

Every home should include intimate places for private relaxation, which is why the design of the master bath matters so much. When it features spectacular views, take advantage of them with a palette that brings in hints of the outdoors.

OPPOSITE: In this Utah house, almost every room overlooks the mountains, including the expansive master bath. The tub is situated to make the most of these vistas. Two-tone travertine tiles add texture underfoot. Motorized shades shield the windows for privacy, while Roman shades add softness. The wood center column of the overhead fixture introduces an element of nature.

ABOVE: A fabric printed with crustaceans introduces warm color and whimsy to this bright, light coastal bunk room. Each bunk includes its own lighting and a niche for books and chargers. In place of closets, hooks and drawers provide storage. OPPOSITE: A room-sized indoor/outdoor rug can be both pretty and practical, especially in a bath by the pool. The seat of the antique bench lifts for extra storage.

ABOVE, LEFT: This simple guest suite renovation features walls in a garden paper and a vanity, repainted a fun shade of green, with a newly added Carrara marble top. An oversized custom mirror helps to reflect light around the room. ABOVE, RIGHT: The vanity color marries the bath to the bedroom, a testament to the power of paint. OPPOSITE: In this ranch house bedroom, a jute rug and a mohair-upholstered headboard contrast plush and rugged textures in two complementary neutral shades.

PATTERN AND TEXTURE

Pattern and texture probably have more power than all of design's other principles and elements to either establish balance and harmony or tip things into discord. Patterns, especially in combination, can so easily yell, "Look at me, look at me, look at me!" Textures are another story. Because we love the calmness that comes from a mix of beautiful textures, we tend to use pattern sparingly, but with an eye for interest. Sometimes a form or a line found in the art or the rugs can energize a room all by itself. That said, nothing can make a space more intriguing than the smart use of one pattern or a carefully selected combination of many patterns with just the right balance of scale and color.

The rug in some instances dictates the largest pattern in the room. If it has an overall design but a very subtle coloration, it generally plays well with other fabrics and finishes. Finding the right blend of organic shapes with geometric patterns, stripes or plaids with florals, calls on all our training as designers. The pleasing solution always involves just the right variation in scale. Sometimes the architecture of the room seems to cry out for the unexpected. This is when we will go out of our comfort zone and select a bold pattern. Suppose there happens to be very little wall surface in a room to hang art; here, a pattern can stand in for artwork. Or, if the space itself lacks character, a paper with a strong personality can ameliorate the flaw. In a two-story gallery in a simple house at the beach, for example, an acanthus-leaf stripe pattern on the walls can enhance the verticality of the space. If there also happens to be an unattractive wood-and-stone combination underfoot that fights every last design effort and is too costly to remove, a wall-to-wall sisal can layer over the eyesore. Its subtle pattern and texture then direct the attention away from the floor to the pattern on the walls. And the effect of the combination is transporting.

OPPOSITE: Layering a smaller, patterned rug, like this antique Oushak, on top of the texture of a room-sized sisal solves the problem when it is impossible to find one rug to fit the room. The bench's distressed finish and rush seat contrast harmoniously with the bed frame's smooth finish.

ABOVE: With a central stair, this entry hall calls for symmetry. It can be a challenge to find pairs of antique consoles, mirrors, and lamps to meet the demands of function and style, especially in a small scale. The gilding on the trumeau mirror and lamp base enhances the effect of the console's aged paint finish. OPPOSITE: A forged-iron tripod table with a polished stone top provides an interesting textural contrast to the embroidered fabric on the antique Sheraton bench and the hand-knotted rug.

As restrained as we generally are with pattern, we tend to employ texture very liberally. Textures add so much warmth and interest to a space. And of course, they invite your touch. With fabrics, we always have our clients handle the cloth and put it next to their cheek to see how it feels. Mohair, for example, is beautiful and indestructible. We love it. But some people find it uncomfortable on bare skin.

Some components, like embroidered fabrics, combine texture, pattern, and color. We are always thinking about the mix, about how to combine rich textures, like woven leather, with smooth ones, like stainless steel, in a way that makes each more interesting. The same is true of our approach to pattern. Difference matters in design. Contrast helps us to see and appreciate each element. It also enhances the combination.

Pattern and texture, though, are not the sole domain of fabrics and wall coverings. They are also inherent features of just about every finish from tiles to flooring to stone to countertops and furnishings. The difference between a hand-planed antique wood floor and a highly polished floor is night and day. They can be the same color, but if one of them has a wonderful texture and one of them is smooth, they will look totally different. Stone is the same. Countertops can have a honed, leathered, or polished finish, each of which offers a completely different look. Think about brick patterns: running bond, herringbone, straight lay, and so on. There are so many options for creating pattern with simple surface materials. These can add so much to a space. Furniture finishes also often have stories to tell. A highly polished piece brings one kind of character. An antique piece that still has its wonderful original patina as well as the nicks and the gouges of use infuses a room with another. That piece is like life. The marks of time are what make it interesting, just like us.

RIGHT: In this dining room, grasscloth wall covering provides an organic, textural backdrop for the large-scale piece the homeowner requested for storage. Refinishing the vintage, mahogany-stained chairs with a white glaze enhanced the woodwork pattern of the chair backs, and offered a vivid contrast to the dark alder, birdcage-base table.

OPPOSITE: A mix of old and new highlights texture in the Lucas morning room. Tables made from repurposed vintage staircase treads speak volumes about age and beauty. The glaze of an antique jar converted to a lamp adds shine. ABOVE: In this sitting room, the artwork's strong blues inspired the accent pillows and ottoman, which also adds texture with its tufted upholstery and nailhead trim.

A room's architectural elements—floors, walls, windows, doors, fireplace, millwork, and ceiling details—establish a foundation of pattern and texture. Paying close attention to the surroundings leads the way in so many design choices.

OPPOSITE: In this renovation, the dining room kept its original high wainscot; painting the existing dark finish white helped to bring the room up to date. With no real space to hang artwork, a bold Christopher Farr wallcovering with a painterly pattern serves the purpose. The chairs' herringbone fabric layers on texture and pattern at an entirely different scale, one that adds to the overall effect without calling attention to itself.

OPPOSITE: In the entry hall of this vacation home on Kiawah Island, sisal that stretches almost wall to wall calms the pattern of an existing wood-and-stone floor. On the walls, a printed grasscloth provides another layer of texture and a contextual reference. An antique table and blue-and-white vases add interest.
ABOVE: In the powder room off the entry, a faux bamboo mirror and a leafy wallcovering suggest hints of the British West Indies. The blackened bronze sconce mounts match the finish of the existing faucets.

OPPOSITE: Glazed woodwork, grasscloth wallcovering, a stone mantel, and wall-to-wall sisal have transformed this study, previously with dark wood paneling and red walls, into an airy, welcoming retreat. A found zebra rug and the husband's favorite antler chandelier add nature's own patterns into the mix.
ABOVE: With its acanthus print, the grasscloth introduces the warm welcome of pattern and texture. The large-scale seaweed prints are fun and a bit unexpected, but also provide a sense of place.

RIGHT: Wonderfully patterned bed pillows make a great impact against the bedroom's palette of neutral solids. The blue-and-white glazed ceramic garden stool introduces a dose of stronger color.

ABOVE: In this Houston master suite, subtle variations in the gray-washed, knotty alder ceiling planks speak to mélange of colors and textures. Polished nickel nailheads create a reflective rhythm on a custom chest wrapped in faux leather. OPPOSITE: A vaulted, wood-plank ceiling gives this ranch house master suite much needed height. Floor-to-ceiling draperies reinforce the verticality. On the footboard, a combination of fabric, wood, and nailheads plays hard against soft.

ABOVE: The complementary patterns of this hand-screened print from Brunschwig & Fils and the china prompted this table setting for breakfast in the Eilers garden. A multilevel centerpiece of antique blue-and-white vases along with hand-blown blue goblets provide the perfect accents. OPPOSITE: Every choice in this bunk room, designed for grandchildren and their friends, is about durability and fun. The indoor/outdoor rug adds a pop of color. The sectional is slipcovered for easy maintenance.

ART AND COLLECTING

The art and objects we love and live with have a way of revealing our souls. This is why we always want to know if prospective clients are collectors. Often, though, we work with people who have not yet found their passion for art and objects. We like to introduce them to these really rich worlds, to suggest and guide them. There is nothing more rewarding than to ignite an interest in something new, to see the eyes light up, to spark the desire to learn all the nuances of whatever it is that has caught their fancy.

It is so much fun to see how a personal appreciation for art and objects develops over the years. Clients whom we introduced to the work of local artists when we were doing their first home twenty-five years ago have grown into very serious collectors. We have also introduced clients to art consultants around the country to guide them through the exciting world of auctions and international collecting. Another client has grown just as passionate as we were about the objects we first opened her eyes to several years ago when we had an entire library to fill. Here we started by bringing in ten beautiful antique boxes, all of different sizes, shapes, and pedigrees, to arrange on the shelves. Since then, she has added so many more to the mix, enjoying the hunt for unique and meaningful pieces.

When we direct our clients to what they might need, typically we turn back to the principles and elements of design. First, we think about form and function, about what shape fits the purpose and the space. We then consider what type of art or object meets the criteria. Sometimes we make suggestions in the hopes that they become a passion. For a pair of very traditional homeowners who needed a grouping of accessories to top the large center table in their entry, we envisioned something tall and cylindrical, a description filled by countless objects. These clients love history and collect American antiques. We proposed an arrangement of trench-art vases thinking they might be the perfect shape, size, color, and design for the spot. Trench

OPPOSITE: The bookshelves of this Houston study display the homeowners' collections of antique duck decoys, turn-of-the-century iron banks, and rare books on Texas. This particular shade of blue not only shows off the collections to their best advantage, but it also makes the cozy space even cozier.

ABOVE: Grouping elements of a collection of American political memorabilia creates a powerful impact in this entry hall. Hammered and engraved, the trench-art vases on the center table provide wanted height and asymmetry, plus an unexpected bit of history. OPPOSITE: Starting from scratch, this client has gradually assembled a collection of rare books on Texas history to mix with the antique clock faces. Arranged against a red wall, the combination brings great personality to the room.

art, made by soldiers from leftover brass casings, was new to them. They loved the idea so much it has become a related avenue for them to pursue as collectors.

There is strength in numbers. Collections, even new collections with just a few pieces, almost always make a greater impact when grouped together. What matters is how each piece relates to the others, and the harmony of the entire arrangement. There is a science of balance, obviously. We place the big blocks first. Then we fill in the spaces around them. As we do, the arrangement starts to tell a story.

Often a client will love the work of a specific artist, but the pieces available at the time do not precisely fit the project. If the artist is open to it, commissioning a new piece or painting can be a fun way to add art that is deeply personal and has special meaning. One of our homeowners loved a particular landscape artist whose scenes depicted places around the country, but not Texas. This couple wondered if he would be willing to create a Texas landscape specifically for them. We called him. He was delighted by the idea. He came to visit their ranch. He took photos. And the experience inspired an entire new series for him, and an heirloom piece of treasured art for the family.

Collecting can be on any level as long as the imagination stays open. We have one homeowner who loves antique maps. Another has a passion for antique silver sugar shakers that she uses for flower arrangements on her dining table. Still another has a treasure trove of found objects—vintage rolling pins and eggbeaters—she inherited from her grandmother; we assembled these objects into two collages in their own shadow box frames that now hang proudly in her kitchen. For another client, we grouped vintage jewelry molds with interesting shapes and textures like art on a wall. There is no limit to the design inspiration that can become an interesting collection.

Art and collections are design's exclamation points. The shell of the room can be beautiful. So can the furniture, rugs, and lighting. But the unique selection of meaningful artworks and accessories is what completes a room and tells us about the people who live in it.

OPPOSITE: For a client who had always wanted an antique secretary, this piece is a cherished find. It holds a few of her many salt glaze pitchers, as well as a set of books custom-covered in the same shade of pale paper with delicate, hand-lettered spines. With these light elements behind glass, the dark wood piece takes on a fresh look.

OPPOSITE AND ABOVE: Flanking the TV cabinet in the Lucas morning room, floating wood-topped iron shelves display a beloved collection of antique iron building banks grouped to make a strong visual statement.
PAGE 114: Atop a serpentine-front chest, a carved wood lamp provides an organic complement to an arrangement of tortoiseshell boxes and a tortoiseshell clock. PAGE 115: This couple has collected, inherited, and been gifted the most marvelous array of antique silver, everything from stunning candelabra to a most unusual epergne the wife loves to use as a centerpiece to a set of goblets that gleam next to their wedding crystal.

If a piece is good and it spoke to you at the time you purchased it, chances are that it will still be good and speak to you thirty years later.

OPPOSITE: When this couple was downsizing from their previous house, there was some concern about whether their new home would be able to accommodate their art collection, which includes a number of large canvases. The renovation, which focused on ensuring they would have sufficient wall space to hang these paintings, included lime-washing the entry's red brick walls to create a pleasing backdrop for favorite works.

RIGHT: In the Lucas master bedroom, his grandfather's coin collection fills the wall behind their bed, a fun and unusual way to bring in family history. Carefully laid out, matted, and framed, the individual pieces, though interesting on their own, take on a totally different kind of visual power as elements of the larger composition. Vaulting the ceiling, originally eight feet, and repurposing the existing beams to give the room loft and definition were part of the overall renovation.

PART II

THE HOUSES

ood design is always complex, especially when the results look easy, comfortable, and right. Behind every finished interior lies an intricate process that requires many tough decisions. Whether the project consists of building a new home, remodeling an existing one, or just doing a single space, it requires us to sort through more choices in a week than most of us typically make in a year. This is one reason the two of us have always valued the importance of our formal design training. It is also why over the years we continue to rely on the principles and elements of design to help guide us every step of the way.

In this section, we highlight several houses that demonstrate our design process for creating interiors that perfectly express our clients' personalities and thoroughly meet their needs. While many of our projects over the course of our careers have been in our hometown of Houston, we have also been fortunate to work on projects all across the country.

The more we travel, the more important we have found it to be that each individual space tells the story of the people who live in it. Listening to our clients, observing their needs, applying our years of experience, and considering everyone's ideas makes all the difference to the design choices we make from the countless options available to us.

At best, a home is so much more than just shelter. This is why we work so hard to create beautiful, workable interiors that provide the backdrops to happy, busy, and productive lives. The five homes on the following pages illustrate what we mean by this. They include several homes in Houston. Some are primary residences for young families and empty nesters. Others are second homes meant to welcome multiple generations and friends. Some are newly built. Others are remodels. One is as far north as the Utah mountains. Another hovers on the Gulf Coast of Texas. All are the result of meaningful collaborations with our unique clients, talented architects, and capable contractors.

In each case, the home is the stage where specific people with distinctive interests and preferences act out the details of their lives and escape the stresses of the day. Our ultimate goal is to make sure these homes become the single most important expression of their owners' passions, preferences, and personal style.

A PERIOD MIX

To create a light, bright, comfortable haven for this pair of empty nesters, we truly started from scratch. The couple wanted their new home to have a French flavor, with old-world touches. They were passionate about incorporating reclaimed architectural elements like wood beams, wood and stone floors, and stone mantels into rooms framed by plastered walls and filled with a mix of antiques, contemporary furnishings, and modern artwork. Developing collections to complement their heirloom pieces was especially fun.

In the entry, a stone floor from an old French monastery provided a wonderful patina; a chandelier with a mix of contemporary and antique components and antique-inspired sconces enhanced the serene atmosphere. In the adjacent living room, we laid a foundation of timelessness using new rugs with an aged look. Here, an antique iron gate converted into a coffee table served as a focus for a conversation area at one end of the room; an antique table used for cutting fabric, a beast in terms of scale, anchored the other. A Swedish cabinet, one of the last pieces we found, punctuated a corner with importance.

Using a soft palette, we created a quiet, glowing atmosphere for the dining room. A pair of antique chandeliers added delicate touches of sparkle overhead. Sconces and a contemporary landscape painting by Bruce Brainard completed this room's mix of yesterday and today.

The kitchen opened through a stone archway. Its harmonious contrast of materials and finishes included reclaimed beams and a wood ceiling, a stone overmantel for the hood, reclaimed concrete tiles for the backsplash, and a glazed finish on the cabinets.

For the master bedroom, they wanted a serene retreat. We established this with soft colors, a custom upholstered sleigh bed, and embroidered linens. A pale palette of iceberg quartzite, a custom mosaic floor, and a simple marble tile carried this calmness into the master bath, where three antiqued Venetian mirrors added a quiet gleam.

The toile of the upholstered headboard inspired the décor of the guest room. Married with a small plaid, it gave the space a French feel. We wove in important family antiques here as elsewhere and freshened the look with lamps made from decorative iron castings.

OPPOSITE: This entry sets the stage for all that follows with reclaimed architectural elements, evocative plaster walls, antiques, and period-inspired French details. An old French limestone floor lays a groundwork of history. The hand-forged stair rail and spindles add to the craft tradition. Period-inspired sconces and a chandelier with a mix of contemporary and antique components balance the quiet envelope with just enough embellishment to create interest without overwhelming.

RIGHT: The couple wanted only one seating group in this expansive living room. A pair of antique armchairs helps create an arrangement flexible enough to welcome both intimate and large parties. Reclaimed elements include the oak ceiling beams, the fireplace mantel and the fireback bricks, and an antique iron gate reworked as a base for the coffee table. Wool sheers soften the light. PAGE 126: A massive antique sewing table anchors the wall at the room's opposite end. Two framed panels of a scenic wallcovering from Gracie hang like art above it. The lamp bases are made from an old column. PAGE 127: With its perfect patina, this antique Swedish corner cabinet, the last piece we found, fully expresses the sensibility behind the room's design.

ABOVE: A pair of painted cabinets flanks the dining room doorway, adding additional storage. The silver service is inherited from the wife's family. The French nineteenth-century gilt-bronze sconce is one of a pair. RIGHT: The couple wanted a pair of antique chandeliers for the dining room, not an easy find by any means. Just before the Sheetrock went up on the ceiling, however, this duo of Italian wood and tole fixtures fortuitously appeared—the dream solution. A pale new Oushak harmonizes with the room's overall lightness of being. A large landscape by Bruce Brainard holds focus on the far wall. The couple found the German silver and rock-crystal candlesticks, circa 1780, in Santa Fe.

RIGHT: This kitchen acquires a feeling of history with reclaimed beams and wood on the ceiling and antique concrete tiles, plain and patterned, for the backsplashes. The large custom hood adds function, architectural definition, and an ingredient of timelessness. Between the floor and ceiling, the color palette centers on pale grays. Done in a slightly darker gray tone finished with an antique glaze, the cabinets add warmth.

ABOVE: Flanked by old iron sconces, an antique door found by the clients creates a focal point on the upper landing. OPPOSITE: A soft, blue-gray plaster calms the master bedroom's walls and vaulted ceiling. A custom, fully upholstered sleigh bed introduces another variation on the French theme. PAGE 134: The pastoral paintings in this guest room are handed down from the husband's family. PAGE 135: The use of toile gives this room a true French flavor. A long bench at the bed's foot is convenient for suitcases.

HOME BASE

This young family with three small children loved their existing 1950s Houston ranch house. When they needed room to grow, though, they opted after serious study to tear it down and rebuild. They wanted their living and dining spaces to have a more formal, established, traditional feel because they entertain a great deal. They also required a casual, more contemporary family room; a wonderfully functional kitchen with an adjacent butler's pantry and a bar; and a home office for her. Their family heirlooms, both furnishings and artwork, were integral to our design process.

At the front of the house, a procession of ceiling lanterns lit a path through the glassed-in gallery to the entry hall, where a custom settee and an antique mirror anchor one wall. In the family room, an apple-green wall made her prized collection of blue-and-white porcelain stand out in a fresh way.

The husband and wife both had happy memories of gathering with their families around a formal dining table for everyday meals as well as special occasions. They wanted to recreate that tradition with their own children, so we found an antique Sheraton pedestal table that can just as easily seat twelve as it can five. A fresh custom chandelier ensured that the room would never be too formal for everyday breakfasts.

Kitchen cabinetry painted a confident shade of blue that appealed to both husband and wife, plus touches of stainless steel, bright brass, and dark wood, brought warmth and definition to the light, practical space that served as the heart of the house. In her adjacent office, millwork finished in the same shade of blue as the kitchen cabinets created a feeling of cohesion.

With white walls and a pale blue ceiling, the master suite took cues from the pool it overlooks. In the master bath, a Biedermeier stool helped establish her vanity area.

Blue was her favorite color, with green a close second, so we used various shades of these two hues throughout. Paler blues and greens mixed with unlacquered brass and some iron pieces brought a serene air to the more sedate spaces, both public and private. Bolder, brighter, more whimsical tones enlivened the relaxed spaces, including the children's bedrooms. Mixing in more modern elements with their antiques gave a fresh spin to the grounding of tradition that they love.

OPPOSITE: Without detracting from the view, a simple runner and repeated bell jar light fixtures from Urban Electric direct the way through the gallery that connects the entry to the master suite; at night, the fixtures create a wonderful glow. The gallery wall provides a perfect spot for displaying portraits of the children painted by a local artist. A vintage etching, a gift from the husband's parents, establishes a focal point at the gallery's end above a brass demilune.

As the old saying goes: "You only have one chance to make a first impression." We believe this is also true for the entry to your home.

RIGHT: This custom settee in the front entry hall works well for many different purposes, including as a place for the children to sit or park their book bags when they are waiting for rides to school; its cutout back responds directly to the circular mirror. **FOLLOWING SPREAD**: A controlled explosion of color draws people into the family room.

138 EXPRESSIVE INTERIORS

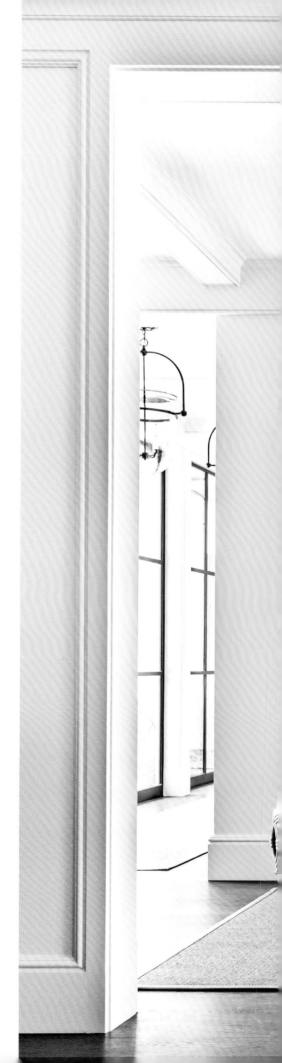

RIGHT: Because this family often uses their dining room for all three meals, natural daylight is just as important to the space as artificial illumination. Multiple windows ensure a beautiful daytime glow. With a vaulted ceiling void of recessed fixtures, the custom chandelier has ample reach and enough candles to create a wonderful evening ambience. The reproduction Khotan rug has a pattern and tight weave that make it more forgiving to spills. The Paul Cézanne print over the nineteenth-century console is a family piece.

RIGHT: It is always fun to work on kitchens for families in which the husband loves to cook because the approach is very pragmatic. Mixing materials—such as wood for the cooktop counters and Carrara marble on the island— helps make the backdrop of the room more interesting. Incorporating shelf space into the island creates much needed (and very handy) storage space for cookbooks. The large, adjustable, counterweight pendant is modeled after Florian Schulz's mid-century Double Posa design.

A master suite should always be a serene retreat. But when the palette is pale, soft, and ethereal, a pop or two of a contrasting color can quietly energize the surroundings.

RIGHT: This custom, upholstered headboard incorporates a keyhole for a fun focal point. Monograms and appliqués, such as these designs from Leontine Linens, help to create an elegant, personalized bed. With two sections, the settee at the bed foot is flexible enough to use for pull-up seating; it also provides a cozy place for the children to hang out with their parents.

RIGHT: In the master bath, his-and-hers counters on opposite sides of the room flank the shower and tub. The tub's pewter finish contrasts nicely with the Carrara marble floors and Grigio Verona marble counters from Walker Zanger. Creating a vanity area at sink height along the wall of cabinets ensures a continuity that keeps the space visually well organized. With a Biedermeier stool at the appropriate height, the area works perfectly for her. Multiple sconces indicate the different functions and add verticality as well as necessary illumination.

ABOVE: Around the corner from the kitchen, the wife's office is bathed in the same blue-and-white palette. Ample, below-counter storage accommodates her files. Built-in shelving serves many purposes, including as display space for the children's drawings and art projects. OPPOSITE: An indoor/outdoor rug fits perfectly in the elder daughter's bedroom. The custom bed frames an upholstered headboard between high posts capped with iron flower finials. Appliquéd patterns on a solid linen ground keep the bedside table simple, but full of charm; the front panel conceals additional storage.

ABOVE AND OPPOSITE: In the son's bedroom, floating shelves replace the usual bedside tables so that a trundle stored underneath the bed can pull out for sleepovers. With three walls of windows overlooking majestic oaks, the room feels like a tree house. Window panels of a leaf-print pattern enhance the effect. A wood-topped metal desk fits perfectly between two windows.

WESTERN VIEWS

This vacation home in Park City, Utah, was an absolute designer's dream for many reasons, not least because it allowed us to develop so many unique elements. The couple wanted the interiors to nod subtly to the style of the West without being overly rustic. Because all but one room featured spectacular views of mountains covered in snow a good portion of the year, the rooms called out for warm, textural finishes and colors. Reclaimed beams, hand-hewn oak, hand-forged iron, textured stone, and wool and mohair fabrics in deep, saturated hues fit the bill. Vintage Moroccan rugs with long pile and simple, abstract designs added softness underfoot; when we could not find older ones in the necessary dimensions, we designed contemporary versions incorporating Native American patterns.

The expansive foyer set the stage for the refined Western palette. Paneled doors hand hewn from reclaimed oak and a custom cast-bronze light fixture with five panels of oversized leaf designs made subtle references to the surroundings. A large canvas by the German artist Eric Peters depicting an abstract American bison welcomed all comers with a direct gaze. An adjacent gallery area with prints from Andy Warhol's *Cowboys and Indians* series introduced a more modern take on the region's past.

Shaped by three walls of windows, the living room called out for the visual heat of crimson leather as well as the rich texture of reclaimed timbers, iron turnbuckles, and handmade custom rugs.

Because the dining room overlooked the motor court, we wanted its walls to provide a meaningful view. Custom wallpaper with a pattern based on Utah's ancient rock art framed the space with a sense of long history.

A warm, cozy paneled inglenook next to the kitchen welcomed skiers after a day on the slopes. It opened directly to the kitchen, with a design informed by this client's love of cooking and entertaining large groups. Light fixtures over the island cast the downlight she wanted for that workspace, as well as the uplight the room required.

The sleeping arrangements included three master suites—one for the owners, and one for each married daughter—as well as two guest bedrooms and a bunk room. With individual fireplaces to shift the focus from captivating vistas, each room brought the rustic-refined motif to the most intimate level with monogrammed linens and hand-forged iron details.

OPPOSITE: German artist Eric Peters hand makes his canvas before he paints, which gives his work a textural presence just as suited to the surroundings as the American bison it portrays. A vintage Moroccan rug introduces elements of the color palette, pattern language, and focus on comfort that characterize the interiors of this mountain house. Copper lanterns by Bevelo, flanking the door, incorporate satin glass for night sky compliance.

ABOVE: A hand-woven runner designed with native American motifs, custom sconces with leather lashings, and a unique wood-and-iron newel post enhance the stairs. OPPOSITE: In one stair hall, hand-carved doors and casings of reclaimed oak define a transition. A series of prints by American artist Cy Twombly creates a dramatic focal point above an antique trestle table. FOLLOWING SPREAD: In the house's hub, a double-sided fireplace connects this family room to the living room beyond. Beneath a console composed of a leather-wrapped fishing rod case on a stand, antique drums add pops of color and a bit of whimsey.

ABOVE AND OPPOSITE: The art and objects help give the rooms the feel of a mountain house with understated flavors of the West. In the family room, *Sitting Bull* from Andy Warhol's *Cowboys and Indians* series speaks to the themes. (Warhol's *General Custer* hangs opposite.) A custom steel pedestal introduces a subtle asymmetry. The reclaimed beams, plaster walls, and stone pillars—the finishes that envelope the room with an appropriate, rustic elegance—were developed with Shope Reno Wharton, architects of the house.

OPPOSITE AND ABOVE: In the living room, monochromatic wool panels with substantial embroidery on the leading edges softly frame windows that look to spectacular views. A custom rug and red leather chairs add warmth when snow blankets the exterior. Balancing the seating group, nesting tables do multiple duty in front of the sofas. In the summer, the mountainside explodes with blooms and vegetation that look so at home arranged casually in a horn vase.

ABOVE AND OPPOSITE: Inspired by the ancient rock drawings found throughout Utah, a custom wallpaper crafted by de Gournay wraps the dining room in meaningful pattern. The hand-fashioned console, custom designed to fit the room's proportions, incorporates some unexpected Western cues. The base features arrow-like legs seemingly shot through the top, with hand-forged iron fletching atop supporting shafts that end in points grounded in protective discs.

OPPOSITE AND ABOVE: The closest room to the ski run, the blue-paneled inglenook with a deep-pile custom carpet, cushy seating, and a continually lit fireplace provides a cozy reentry for those coming off the slopes. Different finishes and interior architectural details help establish the idea that this house has grown and evolved with additions over the years.

OPPOSITE AND ABOVE: The client wanted a kitchen large enough for an entire houseful of family and friends to be together. A custom console of reclaimed wood with clavos-detailed iron corner brackets extends the island counter and creates a visual transition to the family room. A massive beam conceals the hood above the cooktop; behind it, hand-forged straps frame etched steel panels.

ABOVE AND OPPOSITE: In the breakfast bay, ample light gives permission for dark paneling. Custom hand-embroidered trim carries the arrowhead motif from the dining room onto the leading edge of the Holland & Sherry harvest-colored wool drapery panels. Hand-forged flatware feels absolutely right on this vintage table. A combination of rush and wood gives the Gregorius Pineo chairs a very inviting texture.

ABOVE AND OPPOSITE: In the master bedroom, the architectural envelope—mountain views monopolizing three walls, a fourth wall with a fireplace and doors to the sitting room—dictated the bed placement. A custom steamer trunk wrapped in Hermès fabric and trimmed in leather houses a TV that retracts below floor level. Woven to fit a template of the room's dimensions, the distinctive carpet adds warmth to the space. A custom iron surround with leather straps frames the upholstered headboard with rugged refinement.

ABOVE: With open storage and concrete counters, the matching his-and-hers baths adjacent to the bunk rooms easily accommodate numerous grandchildren or guests. OPPOSITE: The bunk rooms' custom carpet mimics the joy of finding feathers underfoot during a summer hike on the nature trail that surrounds the house. The loft at the top of the spiral stairs houses a play area and another pair of bunks.

ABOVE: With recessed heating elements overhead, the outdoor areas of the house are pleasant in all seasons. This one outside the inglenook features stained, wide wood planks above for visual warmth. Three square tables and comfortable chairs by McKinnon & Harris are easy to rearrange for large or small groups. OPPOSITE: Here, the tables are positioned to look directly out over the ski run, which becomes a hiking and biking trail in the summer. FOLLOWING SPREAD: Just outside the lower-level game room, and protected by the bedroom wing, this covered exterior living room incorporates a TV behind the antique deer panels above the fireplace.

ALL ABOUT ART

In homes, as in life, needs and tastes evolve. When the time comes to move or renovate, some choose to start over with a blank slate. Others want to bring the past into the present, refreshing existing pieces but also introducing new ones to create an expressive mix that represents them now. This calculus is always interesting for interior designers. The rooms shown here, from two successive houses, document solutions we have created with one of our clients, a single mother with three children. Designed not quite a decade apart, the interiors chart consistency and change with pieces from previous residences and new selections. (We also worked with her on her first home, which was traditional.) The results reveal her developing preference for furnishings that complement her eye for contemporary art and photography, as well as her love for classic forms that endure.

In choosing the earlier residence, she prioritized walking distance from school because her children were young. She also wanted spaces that offered a beautiful, blank palette for her rapidly growing art collection. (Shortly after we finished, she opened her own gallery.) Reusing as many of her existing pieces as possible, including her draperies and classics from Barbara Barry's collection for Baker and Holly Hunt, we gave them a smart refresh with selective reupholstering, integrated pieces such as kidney-shaped coffee tables and slipper chairs for contemporary spirit and glamour, and added a few new rugs. We also changed the house's existing decorative lighting (far too traditional for her taste), brightened the kitchen, and created serene yet lively sanctuary spaces for her in the master bedroom and bath.

When her oldest recently reached driving age, she moved to a slightly smaller, light-filled residence opening to a courtyard. Because the purchaser of the prior house had acquired all its rugs and many of its furnishings, including the entire living room, the constants here had evolved. Choice new pieces, like the breakfast room's iconic Saarinen table and Vernon Panton chairs and the dining room's Nebula pendant light from Flos, meld with existing, reupholstered favorites and her bold, fun works of art to punch up the rooms' contemporary flavor. Carrying through are her love of color, pattern, and texture—and spaces that celebrate family life.

OPPOSITE: A custom ombré carpet from Stark introduces an artistic element in the entry hall of the client's third home because spatial constraints make hanging art impossible. FOLLOWING SPREAD: Her second house incorporated as many pieces as possible from her first home. For a spirit of contemporary glamour, that living room combined new kidney-shaped coffee tables, slipper chairs, and a Lucite chandelier with refreshed upholstery and existing draperies.

ABOVE AND OPPOSITE: All three of her dining rooms have included this table and chairs, by Barbara Barry for Baker. In this last move, we reupholstered the chairs in fabric that complements all the blues in the room, from the bold ceiling to the new rug's watery hues to the multipaneled painting by Daniel McFarlane. Also purchased for this iteration are the very contemporary Flos pendant light and the sideboard.

RIGHT: Her previous family room was the perfect place for more of her then-existing pieces, including other classic designs from Barbara Barry's collections for Baker and Holly Hunt.

Every move and every renovation offer an opportunity to explore evolving tastes. Classic designs are classic for a reason. They endure. And they mix beautifully with the new.

RIGHT: The kitchen in her prior home called for brightening. Replacing a brick backsplash with an oversized glazed tile and refinishing the island, formerly painted black, accomplished that goal.

ABOVE: Inspired by vintage wallcovering and blown up for scale, a stencil pattern gives the walls of her previous powder room a graphic presence. OPPOSITE: With an Eero Saarinen table, Verner Panton chairs, and Tom Dixon mirror-ball pendant, her new breakfast room is lighter, brighter, and much more modern than the prior iteration of the same room. Interestingly, the photograph of Central Park by Abelardo Morell, which commands the wall, has transitioned between the two in precisely the same position.

OPPOSITE AND ABOVE: Her current library looks out to a courtyard, a green space echoed in a commanding painting by Cleve Gray. Using contrasting fabrics on chair backs and interior seats, as with these wing chairs from her previous library, can enhance the awareness of sculptural form and give it a greater presence. The light fixture overhead adds a more contemporary element. With a tray, any ottoman can do double duty as a coffee table.

RIGHT: Her master bedroom welcomes all the furnishings from her prior home. A *strié* grasscloth from Phillip Jeffries, the Holland & Sherry trim on the draperies, and a new rug from Stark add to the room's symphony in blue. The standing mirror, purchased when she lived in London, comes from her first, more traditional home.

PAGE 196: In her master bath, a beautifully figured slab of quartz centers the tub and provides an interesting background for a piece of contemporary art with a floral theme mimicked by the lamp and the fabric on the surrounding walls.

PAGE 197: The game room in the new home has a controlled explosion of fun, playful color and pattern. Our Lucas/Eilers project designer needlepointed the bargello pillows just for this space.

SUN, SAND, SEA, AND SKY

When our clients came across this beachfront lot on the Gulf Coast in Galveston, they immediately began planning their longed-for second home. With maturing parents and two college-aged children, they wanted a house that graciously accommodated multiple generations and frequent entertaining. They also felt strongly that the style of the architecture should fit in comfortably with the local historical vernacular.

The main level encompasses generous living and dining areas, easy access to fully furnished decks via a wall of double glass doors, a light-filled study/office, a restful master suite, and a functional kitchen with ample space to prepare large holiday meals. The top floor reached by stairs or elevator houses two bunk rooms (one sleeps four; the other, five), a central living/TV area for casual gatherings, as well as the grandparent's suite and another guest room. All the sleeping spaces were given en-suite baths.

The corrosive nature of the salt air and the frequency of major storms dictated many of our decisions, including interior and exterior finishes and fixtures primarily of copper and brass. Throughout, floors engineered of reclaimed oak gave a grounding of subtle grain and texture amplified by intense sunlight. Because of the high degree of moisture, we opted against wallcoverings. Instead, shiplap walls provided durability, especially in the public areas.

The surroundings influenced our color choices, which are rich in the blues of the sea and sky, the neutrals of the sand, and the yellows of the sun. A flat-weave rug with a geometric pattern in a corresponding palette provided the starting point for the design of the living room, as well as a scheme of hues for the main floor that bled organically into the upper levels. Concrete tiles as wainscoting in varying patterns and tints imbued each bath with character; the color choices informed the schemes of the adjacent bedrooms.

We wanted to animate the surroundings with items that our clients love—and that were appropriate to the setting. Given the location, we took a more whimsical approach than we would in the city, assembling folk-art shorebirds, vintage concrete garden ornaments, majolica oyster plates, and wonderful antique soup kettles.

OPPOSITE: Given the close proximity of this beach retreat to the water, Eubanks Group Architects centered the house's spaces around the views. Every last design decision, both interior and exterior, has factored in the surrounding environment, including climate conditions and tidal patterns. In the simple, functional, light-filled entry hall, practical outdoor pavers add pattern and texture.

RIGHT: The living room's color palette pulls quiet hues from the sea, the sky, and the sand. The patterned rug complements the color scheme. Exposed rafters stained a shade of weathered gray draw the eye toward the exterior living spaces, the Gulf of Mexico, and the farther horizon. Solid, textured upholstery and pillows keep the views front and center. Commissioned art panels over the fireplace open to reveal a TV.

ABOVE: A flock of folk-art shorebirds alight on the living room coffee table. **OPPOSITE:** The owners' beloved Cassie happily relaxes by an antique bench, warmed by the sunbeams that stream into the living room. Picture lights above the bookcases add a warm glow at night. The framed art above the bench nods to the story of the indigenous brown pelican brought back from near extinction. Shiplap is a durable, stylish finish for any coastal house; it also allows for movement in high winds.

RIGHT: Constant views of the water make cooking in this kitchen a complete joy. Antique bricks behind the stove offer a reference to this beach community's architectural history and also bring the feeling of age that comes with reclaimed materials into the house. Double-hung windows above the sink counter can be used as a pass-through for outdoor dining on the deck. With its leathered quartzite counter, the island has a distinctive presence.

ABOVE: On the wall between the stairs and the kitchen, an antique industrial cabinet holds majolica oyster plates with an eye-catching glaze. A vintage yard shorebird perched next to it adds a touch of whimsy.
OPPOSITE: Exposed rafters conveniently conceal cable lights to supplement illumination from the six-sided metal-lanterns. In houses such as this one, outdoor furnishings like these chairs from Janus et Cie and the custom metal-top dining table work just as beautifully inside.

ABOVE: Both durable and decorative, concrete tiles in a range of patterns and colors differentiate the upstairs guest baths from one another. OPPOSITE: The vestibule of the master sitting room buffers the master suite from the living room. The husband often works in this space. Positioned to take maximum advantage of the views, this double-sided desk serves a variety of functions.

In every room, it is important to identify the specific spaces for art. When the works that fill these spots have personal meaning, they contribute so much more feeling to the surroundings.

OPPOSITE: The seascapes by the bed, views from the terrace of the house, are gifts painted by talented houseguests. An antique iron window converted to a mirror reflects the light and views. An indoor/outdoor rug provides comfort and function underfoot. The soothing palette brings the colors of sea and sky into the bedroom.

As the old rule says: Spend a night in each guest room to make sure your guests have everything they need. Even when the spaces are not large, they should be well appointed.

OPPOSITE: In order not to compete with the views, this guest room has a sandy palette. Black-out draperies ensure that guests can sleep past sunrise if they wish. An outdoor lounge chair from Palicek moves easily to an adjacent terrace off the dormer.

LUCAS / EILERS 213

ABOVE AND OPPOSITE: In the bunk room's tight confines, a combination of hooks, overhead storage, and drawers replace closets. Pass-throughs between the bunks make for fun sleepovers. PAGE 216: At beach level, an antique zinc trough sink provides a handy place for washing shells; the concrete counter does double duty as a serving spot for the nearby barbeque area. PAGE 217: An upper deck outside the living room and kitchen is another perfect place for alfresco meals.

RIGHT: A covered porch at the other end of the upper deck is furnished for all sorts of activities: morning coffee with the newspaper, lounging, reading, an afternoon nap on the very comfortable sofa, or cocktails watching the sunset. Vintage life rings give this area a fun focal point.

218

PART III
DESIGN LABORATORY

Effective design has many faces—and countless possible solutions. If we are unsure about whether an idea will work, we often try it on our own homes first to see how successful it can be. Our job includes imagining designs for custom furniture, lighting, window treatments, wallcoverings, etc., and then bringing them to life to fill a specific need or add a uniquely expressive component. These one-of-a-kind ideas may not be "tried and true," so mocking them up in our own homes can give us a level of confidence to implement them for our clients.

When trying something new, there is one important rule we always follow: Draw it. Our brains process visuals one hundred thousand times faster than written text. Experience has taught us that no matter how good we might be at spatial visualization, until we put pen to paper (or mouse to monitor), we will not really know if things fit and how they work together. This is why we are religious about doing furniture plans and elevations for all our projects, and for our own houses, too. Design ideas come to life through the sketching process. Once we have fleshed them out on paper, we can see whether or not they really make sense. After all, it is so much easier to move and change things on paper than in the field. A blank floor plan or elevation invites the imagination to explore every last opportunity for design.

We also want all our design choices, both in our homes and in our projects—everything from finishes to furnishings to fabric—to be as sustainable as possible. While LEED status is very challenging to obtain in residential design, we still make sure that we select energy-efficient options and opt for reclaimed materials and products whenever possible. Antiques are as green as it gets on many levels, so we use and reuse vintage and antique pieces. We think hard about how creative we can be in terms of refinishing and painting, etc., to give older pieces new life. We also believe we must give ourselves and our clients permission to purge the things that no longer work in the space or make us happy. When that happens, we know there is always someone else in the family who wants the pieces in question—which is yet another great way to recycle.

LUCAS RESIDENCE

When my husband and I purchased this early-1970s house designed by architect Lucian T. Hood, Jr., we wanted to update the interior but keep its integrity intact. A narrow, two-story, Charleston-style structure, it had a restricted progression of small rooms downstairs. Because we enjoy entertaining and wanted to eliminate bottlenecks at tight doorways, we opened up the dining room into living and keeping rooms, thereby creating essentially one multifunctional space. Moving the utility room upstairs allowed us to garner a larger kitchen. Hanging an interior drapery between the keeping room and dining room gave us the option of enjoying a cozy, more private space when it suited the occasion. Painting the ceilings blue was an experiment to unify the different spaces. I tried five different shades before finding one that I liked, a test this designer only wants to do at home.

The existing brick floors, originally bright red, would never have been my first choice. But I am practical to a fault. And our bricks had some historical significance, as they came from a turn-of-the-twentieth-century house that belonged to Glenn McCarthy, a Houston wildcatter who was the model for James Dean's character in the movie *Giant*. The challenge was to find a way to live with them. One day during construction, I came by to find the floor totally covered in Sheetrock dust. I loved the effect, so we tried a series of lime washes until we got just the right soft gray. To make up for the missing warmth of wood floors, I added touches of wood elsewhere: the living room shelves, a dining room serving ledge, plank ceilings in the kitchen and keeping room, and nineteenth-century doors to front some storage.

Throughout the renovation, the house seemed to tell me how it wanted to be. I would lie in bed at night, thinking about changes. The next morning, I would go to the house to measure, and the idea would just make everything better.

After eight years here, we finally turned our attention to the powder room. There was a new wall covering I was dying to see, and this space was the perfect place to try it. My late father-in-law always called me a "nester." He was right.

OPPOSITE: The house's original traditional bookshelves, which had storage below and topped out at eight feet, felt confining. For my husband's ever-growing library and to display mementos from our travels, I designed wrapped Sheetrock supports and floating shelves, which open up the room and give it a vertical emphasis. Newly introduced ceiling coffers help create interest overhead.

RIGHT: New steel and glass doors by Rehme with custom screens add architectural interest and allow the living room to open up completely to the patio. The antique Persian Malayer anchors the space nicely, but quietly, thanks to its soft monochromatic palette. A pair of nineteenth-century armchairs mixes naturally with our comfortable, clean-lined upholstery. The coffee table base is made from an antique balcony railing. The mantel, redesigned with appropriate scale and proportion, now fits gracefully into the room. One work from my collection of paintings of interiors, a mid-century oil by the married French artist duo Henri and No Seigle, hangs above.

ABOVE, LEFT AND RIGHT: The side table displays of small silver items collected over the years remind us of where we have been and what we have done. I enjoy moving them from room to room. OPPOSITE: This well-used game table fits perfectly into the living room corner. My weekly mah-jongg group enjoys the Mario Bellini iconic Cab chairs that surround it—the most modern designs in our more traditional house—adding a bit of classic tension to the space.

ABOVE: Nineteenth-century French doors with antiqued mirrored panels front a pair of much-needed, newly created cabinets in the dining room. **OPPOSITE**: We found the architectural castings that form the base of the dining table at an antique shop in New Orleans when we were first married. On the host and hostess chairs, wool and raffia throws found in Paris add texture and a pop of color. An antique architect's parchment scale on an industrial pedestal anchors the corner.

EILERS HOME

Our house was new when we purchased it. Given its fine condition, there was no way to justify a major renovation. We moved into it "as is." And we painted because so many of the rooms were in colors we would never choose. The trim throughout was khaki, which we kept. Our new palette for the walls and ceilings warmed up the spaces and provided a backdrop for our collections—the folk art, family heirlooms, china, linens, and all the other things that we love and make us happy.

Almost all our things are inherited, and we probably have way too much. Yet each piece has a story and a history. The challenge is to make it all work. For example, the dining room's trestle table and ladder-back chairs came from my family's farm. The space is way too tight for the furniture, but the room is the way it has to be. If I were drawing it for a client, though, I know I would say something has to go.

Our needs and wants have definitely changed over time. When our children were young, it was so important to have things hold up. When pets enter the picture, things change again. I lecture clients with cats about their fabric choices for the sofa. I could not say how many times I have reupholstered our family room sofa in the years we have had a cat—or repaired a rug because the dog has chewed a corner. These days, I am tired of the constant fluffing of loose back cushions and rethinking it again.

We have waited for things to reach the point of practically no return before we decided to replace them. The back doors—three sets of French doors—were the first to go. From the start, I could not wait to get rid of my kitchen cabinets. This took a while, but they are now the way I always wanted them. Needless to say, I still have a wish list.

OPPOSITE: My house is all about family. In my entry hall, my mother's bow-fronted chest topped by her Satsuma bowl and some of my matchstick boxes feel right at home with a pair of chairs from my great-grandparents' Eastlake parlor set. The Palissy plates pick up on the palette and patterns of the antique needlepoint pillows.

RIGHT: We live in the family room, which is right off the garden where we also spend a great deal of time. The oriental rug inspired the colors of the space. Painting the back of the bookcases in a shade of rust helps make my collections of blue-and-white porcelain and tramp-art boxes stand out.

ABOVE AND OPPOSITE: The secretary in the living room is from my father's office; when I borrowed it for my first show house room, I lit the shelves and lined the back with fabric to make the collections it held pop. My great-aunt's Empire sofa adds such elegant, contrasting curves. I love the combination of antiques with modern art, such as this John Pavlicek print, one of a pair.

ABOVE, LEFT: The gourd-shaped lamp and textured pitcher pair wonderfully with the forms and textures of my favorite tramp-art boxes. ABOVE, RIGHT: Grouped together, a collection makes a powerful visual statement. OPPOSITE: Like every room in the house, my breakfast room is full of memories. My mother's silver rests on an Eastlake chest from my parents' farm that holds all my table linens. The fern collection—two are prints; the others are pressed—brings the outdoors inside.

Acknowledgments

Where do we begin? So many incredible people have made it possible for us to live our dream and to do the work we love. It is such a privilege to create distinctive interiors alongside clients, associates, vendors, artisans, architects, and builders whose friendship and support we dearly treasure.

It takes a village to produce a book, and our amazing villagers have made this journey such an enjoyable ride. Our most sincere thanks to Sandy Gilbert Freidus, Charles Miers, and everyone at Rizzoli for believing in the expressive interiors created by two passionate designers in Houston, Texas. Your support and guidance are appreciated more than you know. The keen eye, discerning judgment, and impeccable attention to detail provided by Doug Turshen and his very capable team were critical to the composition of this book: many thanks for your talent, direction, and enduring humor. Our most humble gratitude to the very gifted wordsmith Judith Nasatir, who "got us" immediately and articulated our design theories so eloquently. And to Stephen Karlisch, our principal photographer, who takes the art of photography to the highest level, we thank you for capturing our projects so beautifully and for making our photo shoots so very much fun.

We are fortunate to have worked with so many talented designers, architects, and mentors over the years, who continue to shape our design aesthetic and reinforce our business ethics. We are thankful for the professional organizations that have provided valued guidance and are honored to be a part of the supportive design community that we hold dear. The vast amount of talent and teamwork that go into each endeavor are a testament to the strength that exists through collaboration. It is our greatest pleasure to explore, sketch, exchange ideas, and then . . . to feel the goose bumps that arise as it all begins to come together.

Every member of our talented Lucas/Eilers family, both past and present, has been instrumental in molding our firm's purpose and creating our body of work. From each gifted L/E designer to our resourceful procurement and management teams, we value the talent, collaborative spirit, and support you have all dedicated to our undertakings. We would also like to thank our beloved mentor, Mary Ann Bryan. It is one of our missions in life to guide and inspire others as thoughtfully as you always directed the two of us.

And we couldn't possibly close without recognizing our immense good fortune in joining forces with our wonderful clients who become like family. We send our greatest thanks to you and to our immediate families and friends, who mean the world to us. You all make life such a wonderful adventure and we are grateful for you every single day.

First published in the United States of America
in 2020 by
Rizzoli International Publications, Inc.
300 Park Avenue South
New York, NY 10010
www.rizzoliusa.com

Copyright © 2020 Sandra Lucas and Sarah Eilers
of Lucas/Eilers Design Associates

All photography by Stephen Karlisch Photography,
except for the following images:

Gordon Beall: pages 22–23, 62

Ryan Ford Photography: pages 70–71

Peter Molick Photography: pages 46–47, 60–61

David Schilling Photography: page 115

Julie Soefer: pages 5, 6, 10, 15, 20–21, 27, 28–29, 30, 31,
34–35, 44, 45, 55, 67, 69, 72, 73, 76, 77, 78, 79, 82, 83,
87, 88, 89, 90–91, 98, 100–101, 105, 107, 108, 109, 111,
114, 130–131, 137, 138–139, 140–141, 142–143, 144–145,
146–147, 148–149, 150, 151, 152–153, 182–183, 186–187,
188–189, 190, 239

Publisher: Charles Miers
Editor: Sandra Gilbert Freidus
Editorial Assistance: Elizabeth Smith and
Rachel Selekman
Design: Doug Turshen and David Huang
Production Manager: Alyn Evans
Managing Editor: Lynn Scrabis

Printed in China

2020 2021 2022 2023 / 10 9 8 7 6 5 4 3 2 1

ISBN: 978-0-8478-6773-8

Library of Congress Control Number:
2020938360

Visit us online:
Facebook.com/RizzoliNewYork
instagram.com/rizzolibooks
twitter.com/Rizzoli_Books
pinterest.com/rizzolibooks
youtube.com/user/RizzoliNY
issuu.com/Rizzoli

ABOVE: The brilliant color of this contemporary Soon-Oke
lacquerware provides a nice contrast to the trio of bronze birds
that surround it. PAGE 239: A simple vase of ranunculus on an
antique book creates a quiet moment. ENDPAPERS: In presenting
design ideas, sketches are worth a thousand words.

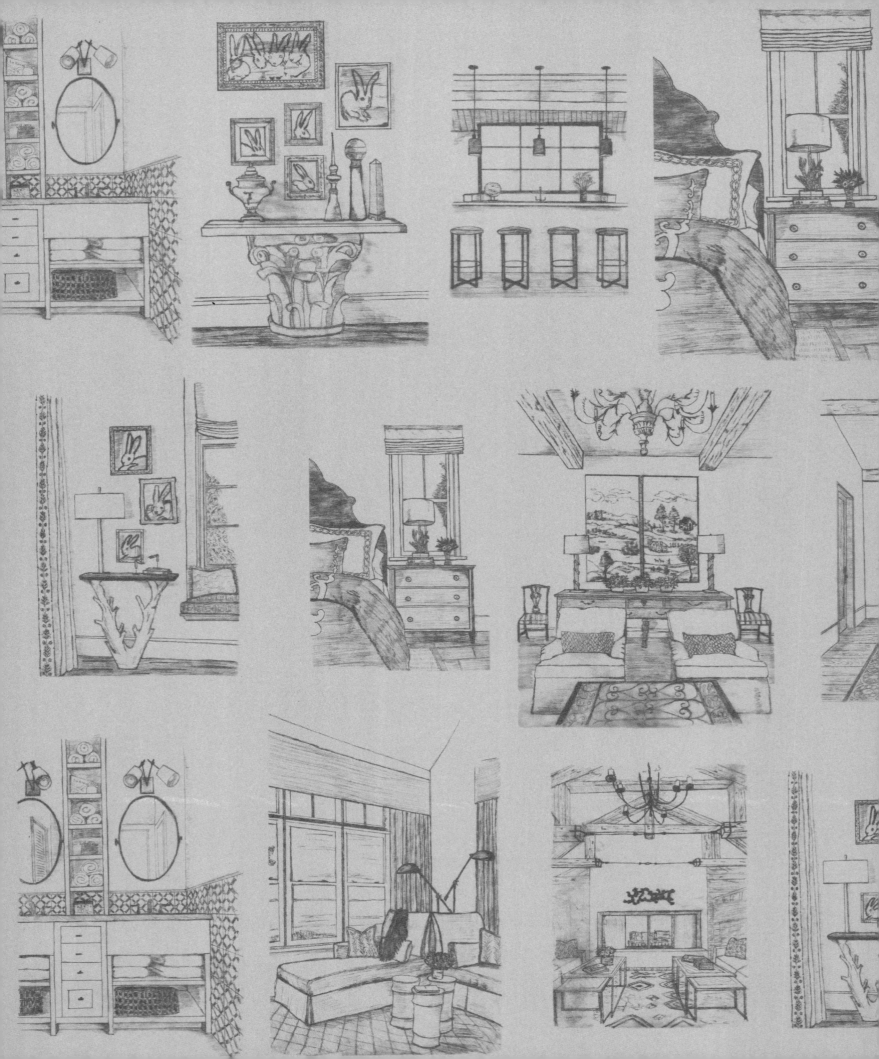